DATE DUE

APR 2 5 2012			
FEB 1 4 2013			
SEP 1 6 2014			

E

BC#9295 $19.95

Pass it Lacrosse

John Crossingham

Crabtree Publishing Company

www.crabtreebooks.com

SPORTS STARTERS

Created by Bobbie Kalman

Dedicated by Ken Wright
For Christa Wright and the Pizza Girls.

Author
John Crossingham

Editors
Kelley MacAulay
Adrianna Morganelli
Robert Walker

Photo research
Crystal Sikkens

Design
Rose Gowsell

Production coordinator
Katherine Kantor

Illustrations
Katherine Kantor: page 5
Bonna Rouse: pages 4, 6, 7, 8, 9, 10, 11, 12,
    14, 16, 18, 20, 22, 24, 26, 28, 30

Photographs
Gemma Williams in association with Texas Men's Lacrosse Club:
    pages 6, 14, 18, 19, 22, 24, 26
Icon SMI: Rick Denham: pages 10, 28; Mark Goldman:
    pages 15 (right), 20, 21; Michael Martin: page 17 (right);
    Max Turner: page 23; Ed Wolfstein: page 29
iStockphoto.com: back cover
© Photosport.com: pages 8, 13 (top), 15 (left), 25, 27
Shutterstock.com: front cover, pages 1, 3, 4, 12, 13 (bottom),
    16, 17 (left), 30, 31

Library and Archives Canada Cataloguing in Publication

Crossingham, John, 1974-
    Pass it lacrosse / John Crossingham.

(Sports starters)
Includes index.
ISBN 978-0-7787-3141-2 (bound).--ISBN 978-0-7787-3173-3 (pbk.)

    1. Lacrosse--Juvenile literature. I. Title. II. Series: Sports starters
(St. Catharines, Ont.)

GV989.14.C76 2008   j796.34'7   C2008-900931-2

Library of Congress Cataloging-in-Publication Data

Crossingham, John, 1974-
    Pass it lacrosse / John Crossingham.
        p. cm. -- (Sports starters)
    Includes index.
    ISBN-13: 978-0-7787-3141-2 (rlb)
    ISBN-10: 0-7787-3141-3 (rlb)
    ISBN-13: 978-0-7787-3173-3 (pb)
    ISBN-10: 0-7787-3173-1 (pb)
    1. Lacrosse--Juvenile literature. I. Title.
    GV989.14.C764 2008
    796.34'7--dc22
                                        2008004849

Crabtree Publishing Company

www.crabtreebooks.com   1-800-387-7650

Published in Canada
Crabtree Publishing
616 Welland Ave.
St. Catharines, Ontario
L2M 5V6

Published in the United States
Crabtree Publishing
PMB16A
350 Fifth Ave., Suite 3308
New York, NY 10118

Published in the United Kingdom
Crabtree Publishing
White Cross Mills
High Town, Lancaster
LA1 4XS

Published in Australia
Crabtree Publishing
386 Mt. Alexander Rd.
Ascot Vale (Melbourne)
VIC 3032

Contents

What is lacrosse?

Lacrosse is the oldest team sport in North America. Two sides compete against one another, trying to score points by putting a rubber ball into their **opponent's** net. Players use **crosses** to catch, carry, and throw the ball.

Lacrosse is a very popular college sport in America.

*Lacrosse was once a Native American sport called **baggataway**. Native North Americans played baggataway to train for battle and as part of ceremonies.*

Three ways to play

There are three different types of lacrosse — **men's field**, **women's field**, and **box lacrosse**. Field lacrosse is played outdoors on grass, while box lacrosse is played indoors.

Men's field lacrosse

Men's field lacrosse is played on a grassy field. The playing area is divided in half by a **midfield line**. Each team has a **defensive area**, where opponents try to score goals. A team's defensive area is also their opponent's **attack area**. Each game has four fifteen-minute sections called **quarters**.

Face-to-face

Each game begins with a **face-off** at the center of the field. During a face-off, one player from each team squats down and the ball is placed between their crosses. A whistle is blown, then both players compete to get the ball to their team.

Ten on the field

There are ten positions in men's lacrosse—one **goaltender**, three **midfielders**, three **defensemen** (defenders), and three **attackmen** (attackers).

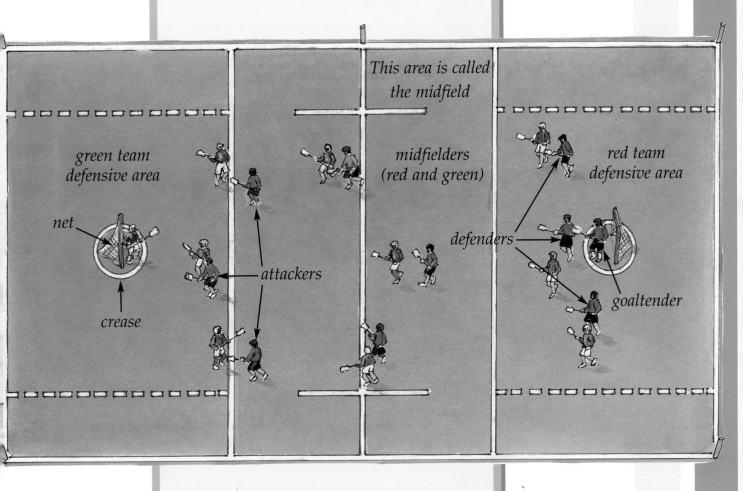

green team defensive area

net

crease

attackers

This area is called the midfield

midfielders (red and green)

red team defensive area

defenders

goaltender

Women's field lacrosse

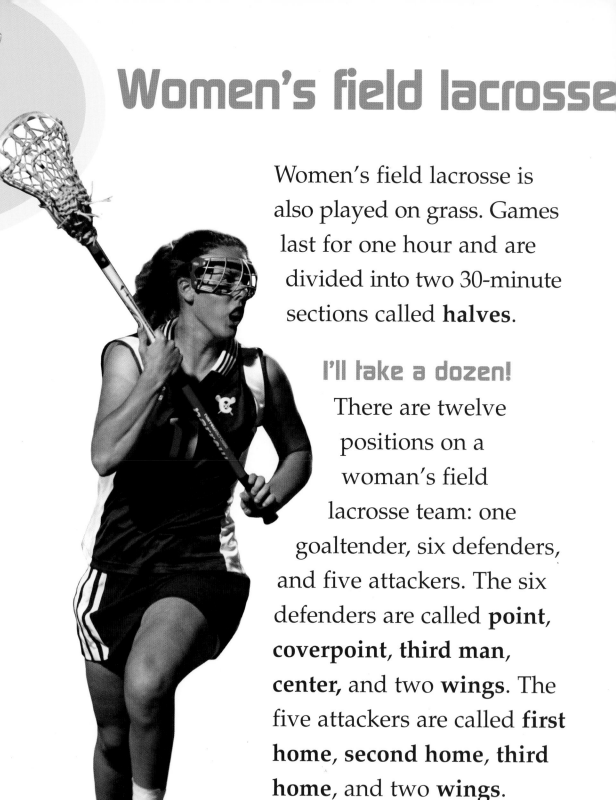

Women's field lacrosse is also played on grass. Games last for one hour and are divided into two 30-minute sections called **halves**.

I'll take a dozen!

There are twelve positions on a woman's field lacrosse team: one goaltender, six defenders, and five attackers. The six defenders are called **point**, **coverpoint**, **third man**, **center,** and two **wings**. The five attackers are called **first home**, **second home**, **third home**, and two **wings**.

Restrain yourself

The two **restraining lines** divide the field into three sections. Only eight players on the defending team and seven players on the attacking team are allowed inside one of these sections at a time.

Women's field lacrosse face-offs are called **draws**. They happen in the **center circle**.

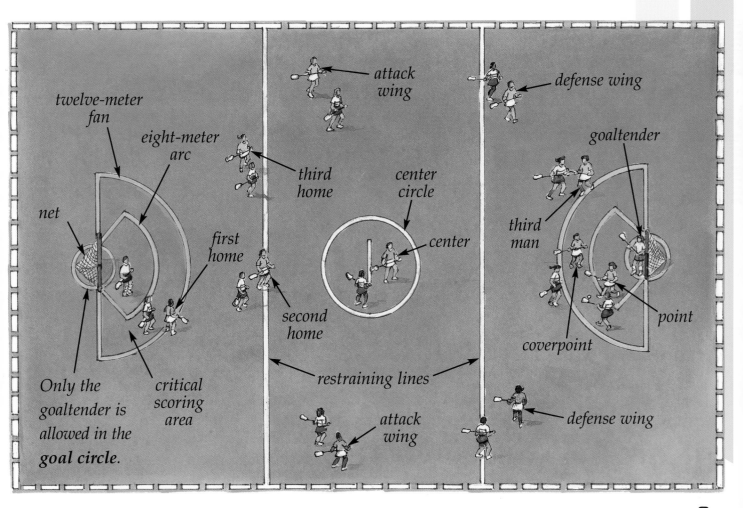

twelve-meter fan

eight-meter arc

net

first home

attack wing

third home

center circle

center

defense wing

goaltender

third man

second home

point

coverpoint

restraining lines

Only the goaltender is allowed in the **goal circle**.

critical scoring area

attack wing

defense wing

Box lacrosse

Box lacrosse is played on surfaces such as **concrete** or **artificial turf** (man-made grass). It is usually played indoors in a building called an **arena**.

Don't delay

Box lacrosse uses a **shot clock**. Once a team gets the ball, it has 30 seconds to get a shot on the net. If the team doesn't shoot, their opponents get the ball. A box lacrosse game is split up into three 20-minute periods.

Six a side

Teams in box lacrosse play with six players on the field at a time: a goaltender, two defenders (called **corners**), and three attackers—two **crease players** and a **point**. Points take face-offs from inside the **small circle** at the center of the field.

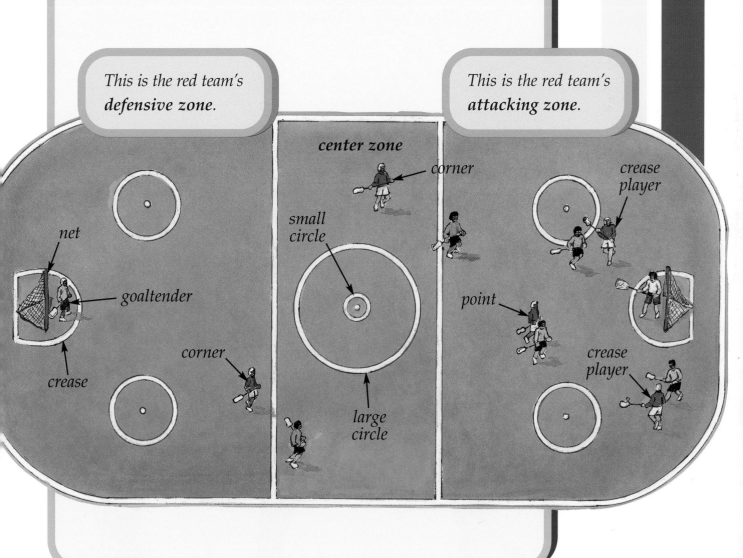

This is the red team's *defensive zone*.

This is the red team's *attacking zone*.

center zone

corner

small circle

net

goaltender

crease

corner

large circle

crease player

point

crease player

Moving the ball

The crosse is the most important piece of equipment in lacrosse. Players use the netting to easily catch, carry, and throw the ball.

Players must be able to keep the ball away from opponents.

Rock the cradle

Cradling is the first skill that a lacrosse player should learn. Cradling is a swinging motion players do with their crosse when carrying the ball. This helps protect the ball from opponents.

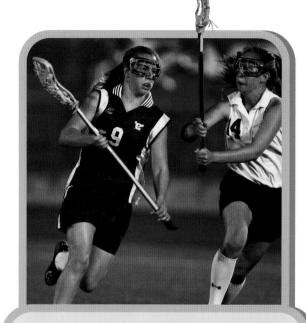

The player on the left is cradling the ball as she runs up the field. She keeps her body between the ball and her opponent.

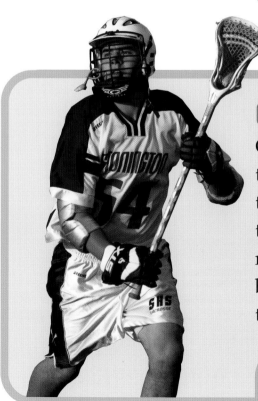

Catch it!

Catching the ball with the stick takes practice. Players must watch the ball closely and follow it into the netting. As the ball hits the netting, players pull the crosse back a bit. This motion helps to trap the ball in the netting.

This player has his stick upright and ready to catch the ball.

Pass and shoot

Quick, accurate **passing** is used to get the ball down field. Short passes are best, as they are difficult for opponents to **intercept**.

Players pass the ball by quickly swinging their crosse toward a teammate.

Sharp shooters

Players score goals by shooting the ball into the net. There are two main kinds of shots in lacrosse — the **sidearm shot** and the **overhead shot**.

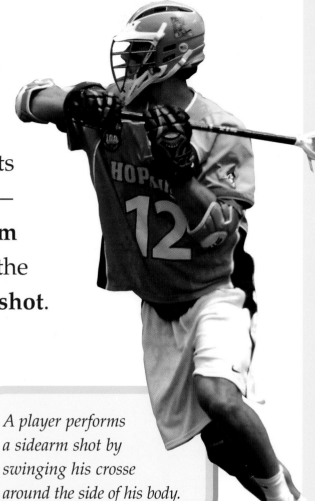

A player performs a sidearm shot by swinging his crosse around the side of his body.

The overhead shot comes from over the shoulder. This shot is the fastest and hardest one in lacrosse.

The goaltender

The goaltender's duty is to keep opponents from scoring on his team's net. Lacrosse shots move very fast, so goaltenders need to have quick **reflexes** to stop the ball.

Goaltenders' sticks have an extra wide netting. This large netting helps them catch shots.

Ready and willing

Box goaltenders and field goaltenders use different **stances** to protect their nets. They also wear different protective equipment.

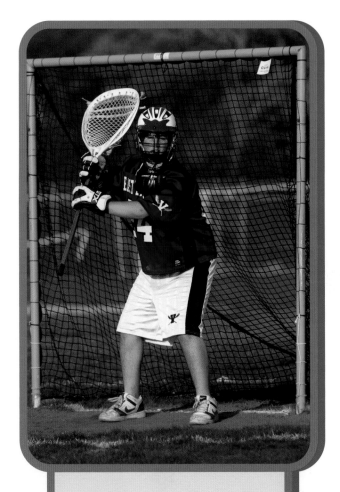

Field lacrosse nets are taller, so field goaltenders usually stand up straighter. They hold their sticks upright, and wear much less padding than in box lacrosse.

Box lacrosse nets are shorter than the ones in field lacrosse. Box goaltenders crouch low to protect their net and hold their crosse pointing down.

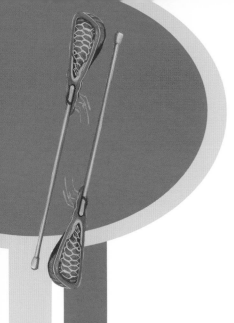

The defenders

Field and box lacrosse defenders all have the same job. These players guard and **check** the opposing attackers to stop them from scoring goals.

*In men's field lacrosse, defenders can use a longer stick for extra reach. These players are called **longsticks**.*

Check it out

In men's lacrosse, players are allowed to body **check** opponents. A body check is when a defender uses his body to try and knock an opponent with the ball to the ground. Women's lacrosse is a non-contact sport.

Defenders always try to stay between an attacker and the net. This position keeps the defender's body in the way of an opponent's shot.

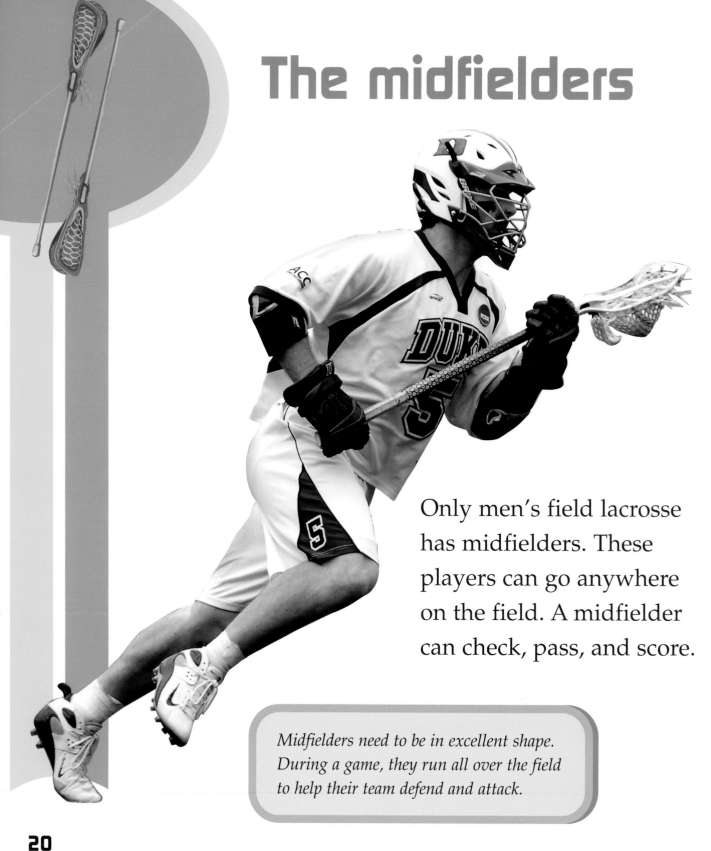

The midfielders

Only men's field lacrosse has midfielders. These players can go anywhere on the field. A midfielder can check, pass, and score.

Midfielders need to be in excellent shape. During a game, they run all over the field to help their team defend and attack.

Well organized

Midfielders use catching and passing skills to help their team score goals. When a midfielder gets the ball, he passes it quickly to an attacker, who tries to score a goal. When his team is attacking, the midfielder remains ready to run back to the defensive area to block shots.

The attackers

Attackers are fast and **agile**. These players are chosen for their position because they have the quickest, most accurate shots. Attackers pass the ball to one another to get around defenders and shoot at the net.

*Attackers use **fakes** to get around defenders. A fake is when you start moving one way, and then switch direction to confuse your opponent.*

Attackers practice catching and shooting often. These players need to be able to move the ball quickly and accurately.

From all directions

Different attackers shoot from different areas around the net. The center attackers stay close to the front of the net. Wings shoot from the side of the net.

Rules and referees

All lacrosse games have **officials**. They watch over the games to make sure all of the players and coaches follow the rules.

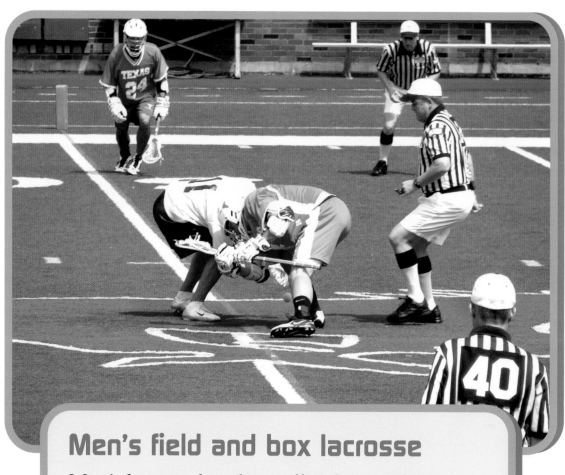

Men's field and box lacrosse

Men's lacrosse has three officials—a referee (the head official), a field judge, and an umpire.

Women's field lacrosse

The official in a women's lacrosse game is called an umpire. When the umpire blows her whistle, every player (except the goaltenders) must stop moving.

Foul play

When players break a rule, they commit a **foul**. Common lacrosse fouls are **slashing**, tripping, or pushing another player from behind.

Penalties

In men's field and box lacrosse, players who commit fouls are given **penalties**. A penalized player leaves the field for a period of time. The player waits in the **penalty box** until their penalty is over. In field lacrosse, penalties last for one minute. In box lacrosse, most penalties are two minutes long. During the penalty, the other team has a **power play**.

Take it, it's free!

In women's lacrosse, fouls are punished by giving the other team a **free position**. With the free position, a player can pass or even shoot without being checked. All players on the punished team must stand 13 feet (4m) away.

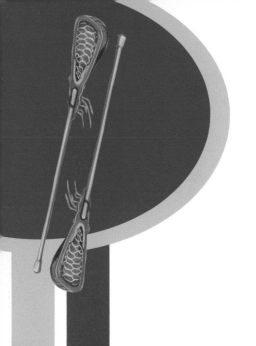

Lacrosse leagues

There are two professional lacrosse leagues in North America. The **NLL** (National Lacrosse League) is box lacrosse, while the **MLL** (Major Lacrosse League) is field lacrosse.

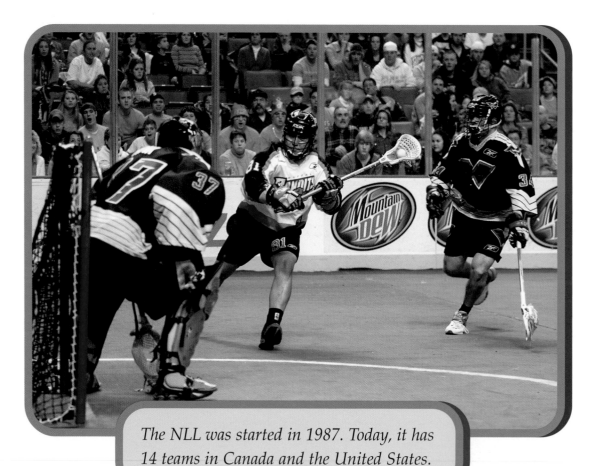

The NLL was started in 1987. Today, it has 14 teams in Canada and the United States.

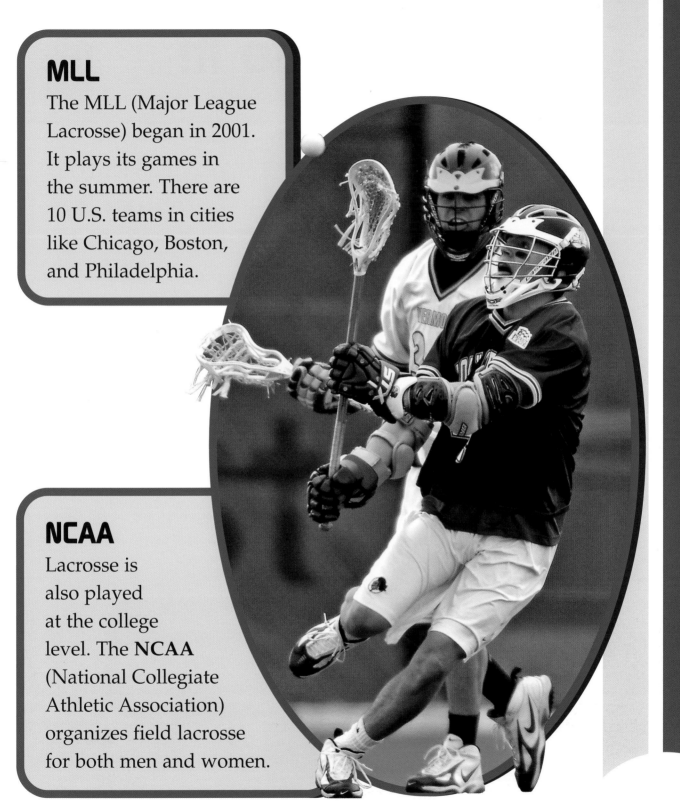

MLL

The MLL (Major League Lacrosse) began in 2001. It plays its games in the summer. There are 10 U.S. teams in cities like Chicago, Boston, and Philadelphia.

NCAA

Lacrosse is also played at the college level. The **NCAA** (National Collegiate Athletic Association) organizes field lacrosse for both men and women.

Get into it!

Do you want to try playing lacrosse? Chances are there is a league that you could play in. Although lacrosse is more popular in some parts of North America than others, you can probably find a team to join near you.

There are lacrosse leagues for many age groups. All you have to do is join one!

Just for the fun of it

Even if there isn't a league in your area, all it takes for a game of lacrosse is a few crosses and some friends. Try finding lacrosse equipment second hand. You'll save some money as you learn to play the sport.

Glossary

Note: Some boldfaced words are defined where they appear in the book.

agile To move quickly

check To knock or bump a player's stick or body to get control of the ball

concrete Hard cement

crosse A stick with netting on the end that forms a pocket

intercept To catch the ball that is being passed between opponents

officials People who make sure players follow the rules

opponent A player on the other team

power play When one team has the advantage of having more players on the field

reflex An action that is not controlled

slashing Swinging a crosse at another player's body

stance The way a player stands

Index

Printed in the U.S.A.